RANDY MEULMAN

NO FEAR IN LOVE

outskirtspress

DENVER, COLORADO

Table of Contents

Introduction...i

Chapter 1: Love Defined......................................1

Chapter 2: The Author of Fear 7

Chapter 3: The Choice.......................................12

Chapter 4: Knowing the Voice of God 17

Chapter 5: The Voice of Evil 26

Chapter 6: Faith and Courage 31

Chapter 7: Spiritual Warfare..............................38

Chapter 8: Transformation from Fear to Love 45

Chapter 9: Loving Ourselves 53

Chapter 10: Suffering.......................................58

Chapter 11: Hall of Fame..................................63

Chapter 12: Where Do We Start?.......................68

Chapter 13: Power to Change 72

Chapter 14: Observations and Opinions 77

Special Thanks 83

To

Jim Moore – I miss you, buddy.

Introduction

We live in a world that is filled with fear and growing more fearful daily. Just the other day, there was a terrorist attack at the hands of religious extremists, and the news media followed this tragic event, covering each phase in minute detail. Natural disasters seem to be on the increase, along with violent crimes. Suicides are now commonplace, even among youths, while disease, accidents, and wars multiply, and there seems to be no end to the death and corruption on this broken planet. The news media faithfully brings each tragic event into our homes, while we willingly feed at the trough of human despair. Feeding at this trough adds meaning and diversion to our own lives, while we desperately try to escape our real fears, which lie just below the surface of our consciousness. We push down and bury these fears that haunt us, that keep us in bondage, while our lives seem sterile and devoid of real life and love.

In this world of fear and confusion, there stands a simple truth that defies logic. There is no fear in love! None at all! That may be a hard statement to embrace, especially if one has never experienced real love. Nevertheless, the fact remains that there is no fear in love.

When you are filled with the love, the world looks very different to you. Love marks the dawning of a new day. Peace resides in the soul of your being, which becomes unshakeable. You feel lightness in your step, which wasn't there before. Everything can be crumbling around you, yet you feel strangely untouched by these problems. You feel compassion for those who are suffering, but you also know that all things work together for good, because that is the way love works. In love, our biggest mistakes are forgiven, and our guilt and regrets are washed away. In love, we find there is no fear of death or loss, because love transcends death. Death becomes the illusion, because we know death has been swallowed up by love. This transformation can come only from within and is found only in the Spirit of love. One cannot find this love through achievement or by human effort. One cannot buy this kind of love, regardless of one's wealth. This love is available only as a gift, to be received by anyone who truly wants it. The question becomes "Are we ready for love?"

1

Love Defined

Many years ago, I was on a flight leaving the island of Kauai in Hawaii. At some point, all of a sudden I was literally transported from the consciousness of this world and ushered into the realm of another dimension. That dimension was the presence of God. I have no recollection when on that flight the event occurred. I was simply transferred from one reality to another, and I witnessed things I didn't believe existed. Actually, at the time of this occurrence, I didn't believe much of anything. I do know that I had all I'd ever wanted from religion and the god most religions worship. This experience marked me for the rest of my life, and I have never been the same. At that time, I knew virtually nothing about real love. It has been more than twenty-nine years since that event took place, and I have spent hundreds of hours trying to explain what it was like to actually be in the presence of God. After all of my attempts to describe my experience, I have not been able to find one word that comes close to conveying what I felt.

"I was suddenly surrounded with inexpressible light and love. The magnitude and the intensity of this energy force were unfathomable. I experienced an infusion of unimaginable joy and Glory. It was an energy of pure love and radiant beauty, magnificence of splendor, surpassing all measure of life as I had known it. Need or want did not exist in this presence, and time had no meaning. I could have rested in that Glory for ten thousand years and never wanted for anything. The majesty I beheld was not of this world. This dimension I had entered was beyond human comprehension or our wildest imagination. This was life and Glory without end."

I think it's best to realize that when we talk about love, we are dealing with a mystery so big, it transcends language. We won't be able to put love in a box. The reason for this is that God is love. God doesn't have love; He is love. I have discovered for myself that no real love exists apart from Him and His goodness. From a human perspective, we have tossed the word *love* around to a point where it has very little meaning. The love that I am writing about transcends death in such a way that it becomes the resurrection. This love swallows up death. The love I am writing about is the very Spirit of God, which can reside in us. There is no fear in this love.

After my trip to Kauai, I returned to Dallas, Texas, where I lived at that time. I was a bit disoriented, and the world looked very different to me. For years, I had wrestled with the god of religion, and I was angry with that god. I not only questioned the goodness of god, but couldn't count the times I'd railed against that god. After this experience, I clearly knew I didn't have a clue Who God was. Once you have been in the presence of God, you will never again question His loving goodness or majesty. I wanted to know more about this Being into Whose presence I had been ushered. But where does one start? Where was I to go?

At that time, I was a businessman, and I often traveled

outside of Dallas on appointments. One day, on such a trip, I was driving, and I was searching for a channel on the radio, trying to find some music, when a man's voice came over the speakers. He was talking about the God Who loves us uncon-ditionally. Normally, I would not listen to this type of program, but on that day I was drawn to what he was saying. He was talking about the Holy Spirit. He said the Holy Spirit is the very Spirit of Christ and that the Holy Spirit is the love of God that dwells within us. This Spirit could heal our pain. This Spirit would never violate us in any way and was a gentle place of shelter. The absolute power of this Spirit is love, and fear cannot exist in its presence. The man's words had a ring of truth, because of what I had witnessed on my return flight from Kauai, and I wanted to know more. I determined to find this Holy Spirit, even if I had to make it my mission in life.

I attended all kinds of churches and conferences in search of the Holy Spirit. I wanted this presence to fall over me or come into my life and heal me. I needed healing. On the out-side, I didn't appear as though I needed healing. I had money and the things money could buy. I was with a good-looking woman and enjoyed hobbies that often filled my days. I was in good health and was a former athlete. Yet on the inside, I was running on empty, and fear gnawed at me from every corner of my existence. I was dancing as fast as I could, to a song that had no music. In my pursuit of the Holy Spirit, I found all kinds of people who could talk about the Holy Spirit, but these were just empty words to me. Where was this Spirit, and why couldn't I find it? Was there something wrong with me? Was I not good enough? After several months of searching, I concluded that my search was in vain. The God Whose pres-ence I had been ushered into was nowhere to be found. Then, on one particular Sunday morning when I was sitting in my beautiful home, working on my second pot of coffee, smoking one cigarette after another, and totally stressed out on life, the Holy Spirit fell over me.

"In those precious moments, I felt as if I were wrapped in a cocoon of love, and I knew I was unconditionally loved. It was as if a bubble of grace had fallen over me, and every cell in my body was at peace. There was no need or want in me. In this blanket of love, there was no fear or anxiety. I was whole. I was completely aware of my surroundings, and I knew I lived in a world full of pain, disappointment, and heartache, motivated by fear. Yet these elements had no hold on me. I understood perfection, which is connected to love, and all of my flaws and shortcomings were washed away. This was the Spirit of God that had come over me. Several minutes passed, and when the Spirit lifted, I was left in a very quiet place."

Of course, this brief encounter was short-lived, and I returned to the daily challenges and frustrations of life. At that time in my life, I wanted God to fix and heal me, and I was hoping He would do that without my having to make choices to change my life. Over the years, I have learned that God doesn't work that way. God works in relationship with us, and we have to be willing to be open to love. I have come to see that I have to invite the Holy Spirit into my world to teach me to love. So many times I find myself with no capacity for love, and I need to be able to see people through His eyes. There are even more times when I have to ask God to deliver me from myself, so that I can love. For me, personally, to really love another person is impossible if I am not connected to God. It is God working in me that gives me the power to change through love.

In one very real sense, the whole purpose of our existence on this broken planet is to grow in love. Everything else—and I mean everything—we own or possess, we leave behind. The only thing we take with us is love, because love never ends. Love goes with us; the rest stays behind.

Before we attempt to define love, let's first examine the purpose of love, which will reveal the true nature of love. We live on a broken planet that for the most part is ruled by fear. If one does not have the eyes to see with love, there is good reason for that fear. Without love, death stalks all of us. Without love, there is no resurrection. But the truth is, God so loved the world that He gave His only Son that whoever believes in Him should not perish but have everlasting life. In Christ, God swallowed up death, so in reality we have nothing to fear—but fear is overcome only through love. Love comes to us from God, and the way this works in our lives is through our relationship with Him in the Holy Spirit. The purpose of the Holy Spirit in our lives is to help us grow in love. Jesus came so that you and I could really live. If your life is filled with love, you know what it really means to live. First, there would be no fear in your life, because there is no fear in love. You could look death right in the face and smile because death has been overcome by love. It is the fear of death that paralyzes us, when we come to the transition of leaving this broken planet for Glory. Another purpose of love is forgiveness. Forgiveness is possible only through love. Christ took all of our unforgiving nature, jealousy, hatred, and selfishness onto Himself and imparted His life to us in the person of the Holy Spirit, so that we can forgive. We can forgive only if we are connected to love. Love is also patient and kind. Love is not boastful or arrogant. Love does not rejoice in harm to another. Love bears all things that are good. Love seeks what is just and is full of gentleness. We have finally come to my definition of love for the purpose of this work. Love is that healing energy force in our lives whose purpose is to promote life and growth and freedom from fear.

Growing in love is a process, just like any other form of growth. So many people in this country and around the world desperately want to be loved but at the same time seem incapable of loving themselves and others, and it's not because they haven't tried. They are running on empty, and fear stalks their lives, as it did with me for a great deal of my life. If you truly want to be free of fear and experience the sense of wellbeing that comes from love, I have some very good news for you. You can find what you are looking for, which is the kind of love that surpasses human understanding. I am not talking about self-sacrifice or mustering up the willpower to do better with empty commitments and promises. I am talking about opening yourself up to the God Who absolutely loves you just as you are, with all of your flaws and shortcomings—a God Who wants you to open your heart to Him.

2

The Author of Fear

On that same flight, leaving the island of Kauai many years ago, in which I was carried into the Presence of God, I also had the opposite experience. At some point, I was literally transported from the consciousness of this world and ushered into the realm of a strange dimension. That reality was Hell. I believe it is important to mention that at that time in my life, I didn't believe in Satan, demons, or a place called Hell. I also believe it's crucial to state that the revelation of Hell posed no personal threat to me, but the revulsion and absolute horror of what I witnessed seemed more than my soul could bear. For months after this experience, I earnestly asked God to erase those memories from my mind. Nothing of God or goodness was found in this place of darkness. Love, compassion, and hope did not exist. Hell is devoid of all meaning, with a sense of unspeakable death that oozed a type of consciousness with nothing to dull or diminish the terror. There was no escape of any kind, and the experience seemed like a surreal nightmare at the time. On this broken planet where we reside, I have witnessed people who feed off human misery and fear. There are those who feel empowered when others cower before them, but not in Hell. There is no power in Hell. In the Hell I saw, there was nothing to feed off. This was a place of torment, absent a feeding frenzy. Words cannot begin to describe this place of agony, of weeping and gnashing of teeth. To be separated from the love and goodness of God is absolute, unspeakable death. It is a state of being of total hopelessness.

Several Hours before This Revelation Occurred . . .

The year was 1987, and I had been retained by members of a Dallas business firm to negotiate a business settlement with a partner who lived on Kauai. The Dallas firm wanted this partner out of its organization. The people who hired me were skittish and evasive, emanating a sense of fear when talking about this partner. They conveyed underlying anxiety and un-easiness when discussing the negotiations. I could not discern what was bothering them, but I sensed an atmosphere of fear. I personally did not care about their fears or apprehensions. I was a former sergeant in the Marine Corps and had spent fourteen months in Vietnam. I was also a former police officer, and I was highly trained in the art of self-defense, along with weapons training. I did not believe in intimidating anyone, and others did not intimidate me. I would soon discover how completely wrong I was.

When I first met with the partner who lived on Kauai, I was completely surprised by his demeanor. He seemed pleasant enough, and his manner was unobtrusive. I couldn't for the life of me understand what those who employed me had feared. The man appeared harmless to me. We started with small talk, discussing the state of affairs in the world. As the hours passed, however, I noticed a disturbing arrogance in much of his thinking. He was also extremely self-righteous and judgmental toward those who had hired me, claiming they were liars and thieves. He was emphatic that lack of productivity was bringing the franchise down, and he felt that the solution called for sacrifice. As more time passed, his anger built. He felt betrayed. I tried to remain as objective as possible, but I was growing tired of this individual. Nothing I said moved the negotiations forward, and a certain banality about this man was evoking my contempt. Several hours had passed since our initial contact, and I could see we were going nowhere, but it was more than that. There was something very wrong about this man, but I couldn't put my finger on it. Finally, when I couldn't stand any more of him, I just went for it.

"What sustains you?" I asked him, point blank.

"What do you mean?" he replied, with surprise in his voice.

"I have always been fascinated by human motivation," I said, "why people do what they do. When I listen to you, I wonder what keeps you from blowing your brains out?"

I meant every word of this. He just smiled at me with a sly, knowing look, and the words slid smoothly from his mouth. "I have a symbiotic relationship with the higher spiritual powers, and they are not good; they are not human." His eyes narrowed. "They serve me, and I serve them. We have a relationship based on mutual respect."

When he spoke, there was a force in that room that I couldn't understand at the time, but I knew what he was saying was true. As crazy as it seemed to me, I knew it was true.

"Our business has terminated," I informed him, in no uncertain terms.

I am not going into specific details in this book about how I escaped from this situation, but I will tell you that it would read like a James Bond novel. This individual had carefully planned a trap that I fell into and had turned demonic forces against me. I experienced fear like I had never known before. There were moments when I felt as if my flesh would melt off my bones, and I thought I was going to die. I was caught in the middle of some horror movie, only this was real. I could not grasp the overwhelming mental and emotional grind I was going through. There was something so inhuman in what I was experiencing. After I finally escaped and was on the plane heading to the main island, I was ushered into the realm where those who choose such an existence go. That dimension is Hell.

After I returned to Dallas, one of the partners confessed to me that he didn't think I was going to make it back alive. There is no doubt in my mind that if the Spirit of Christ had not been in me at the time this happened, I wouldn't have made it off that island.

The man on Kauai who conspired against me by using demonic forces was a weak shell of a man. He possessed no power or authority, in and of himself. My mistake was that I was thinking in human terms, because I knew that man-to-man, I could have kicked his ass all over that island. But this wasn't man-to-man, and maybe nothing really is. I do know that within myself, these crushing malevolent forces of fear would have destroyed me. We are all involved in spiritual warfare, whether we believe it or not.

I realize this is not a pretty bedtime story, but I have some very good news for those who feel any fear after reading this. In this war we are all involved in, Satan and all of his demons are completely defeated in Christ. I certainly wished I had known that bit of information some twenty-nine years ago. I would have handled the situation far differently. All of the tough guy stuff I knew was actually working against me, and that was why I had my butt kicked by that shell of a man and those demonic forces. When it comes to fear, we totally want to trust in the love of Jesus, because Jesus has absolute authority over the spirit world. Being a tough guy has nothing to do with overcoming fear.

If you are anything like me, you probably have many questions that remain unanswered. I personally hate living on this broken planet, where fear seems to rule. I know I was created for so much more. But there are eternal questions being answered here, and our choices are involved in this evolutionary process. The true life and Glory we seek will ultimately be found on the other side, in that place where all will be made new. There will be no more tears, pain, or suffering, and death will be no more. So, in one sense, the whole purpose of our existence on this side is to grow in love. In a very real way, we can experience that resurrected life right now on earth, and our fears will be transformed by love. The love accompanies us, as we leave our fears behind.

3

The Choice

Growing in love is a process, and that process is essentially one of letting go of the old, in order to make room for the new. Ever since Adam and Eve chose to find meaning and life independent from the God Who loved them, fear has reigned in the human race. If you look within yourself, you will discover two natures, and you will also find that these two natures often war against each other. At the core of the old nature, you will find a selfish, willful desire that stands in opposition to love. The old nature wants things my way and has little regard for others. I have to smile when I hear people talk about the innocence of children, as if by some magical process small children are corrupted by society as they grow older. Most of the people who think children are innocent have never had or raised children. For certain, they have never met my little granddaughter, Anne, whom I dearly love. Whenever I think of Anne, I cannot keep myself from smiling. There is no doubt this beautiful little girl has the Meulman gene. I know it would take someone like my daughter to raise this little girl. The child would bury the faint of heart.

When Anne hit the terrible twos, her mother—my daughter—knew she had her hands full. Of course, as grandparents, we find that sort of behavior humorous, because we now get to watch our grown children battle their way through raising their own. Just yesterday, my daughter called me, exasperated, and at the end of our conversation, she said she hoped that one day Anne would be fruitful and multiply. Payback! I had to laugh because Anne takes after her mom, and her mom takes after me. Yet the truth of the matter is, those battles that start with the terrible twos follow us all through life, and that willful selfishness at forty is not cute, the way it is at age two. If we are truly growing in love, giving up the old nature is a lifelong process.

Facing our fears is not easy, even when we know God loves us, but facing our fears before the monster god of most religions is next to impossible. The God I know and I'm writing about won't judge or condemn us. We have been perfected by the finished work of Christ. God is not angry with us. He doesn't guilt us, nor does He have any desire to punish us, but we have to make the choice for love and life. God does not sentence anyone to Hell. Those who are in Hell are there by their own choice. God has provided everything for our salvation, but the fact remains, we have to choose. Here is the really good news. If we want to grow in love and overcome our fears, we don't have to hide anymore from Him. We can talk to Him about anything, and He will not be angry or upset with us. He wants to heal us and deliver us from our fears. He wants all of us to really live and grow in love.

Thinking about facing our fears is very difficult, and we all have a tendency to live in denial. If I really tell you who I am, if I am totally honest and open with you and expose my deepest secrets, you won't love or accept me. Most of us, at one time in our lives, have trusted a good friend or someone we dearly cared for and took the chance, at great risk, of baring our souls, only to have that person reject or judge us. It's very easy after having that experience to slam the door shut and not open it again. I promise you that this rejection or judgment you felt will never happen to you when you talk to the living God, Who unconditionally loves you. Never!

All of the fear that plagues us is ultimately the by-product of being separated from the God Who loves us. The god of this world and the gods of most religions rule by fear. These gods know nothing of love. The god of this world is a liar and, in reality, has no power over us when we trust in the God of love. But we still have to make the choice, and courage is required. If you stay trapped and submit to your fears, you will forever remain in bondage.

We have all kinds of fears that plague us, and some fears are more rational than others. One of the most common fears is the fear of death, for ourselves and the ones we love. We fear failure and rejection. We fear that we will run out of money, or we fear getting sick. We fear being alone and growing old, and we even fear being afraid. We fear boredom; we fear we won't be good enough or that we don't look good enough. We fear we might ruin our children's lives, and we fear God because of our past and present mistakes. We fear judgment day. We also have irrational forms of fear that are more difficult to understand, such as the fear of committing an unpardonable sin or being forced to do something we don't want to do. Some people fear losing their minds. Others fear crossing large bridges, some fear heights, and there are people who fear leaving their homes. There are people who are afraid of their sexuality, those who are afraid of snakes, and those who fear violence and being violated. A dear friend of mine told me that she had a beautiful marriage and a privileged life and feared every day that she was going to lose it, because she was too happy. There are women who fear their husbands and husbands who fear their wives. There are people who fear demons and demonic possession.

The list of things we fear is almost endless, and the one thing all of our fears have in common is that they prevent us from living. All of the fear in our lives points to a lack of love. There is no fear in love. When it comes to our more rational fears, which make perfect sense to us, we think it's okay to have them. Some people even find their fears comforting. Many people hang onto their fears because they give meaning to life. If I'm worried about my finances, it takes my mind off my terrible marriage. If I'm constantly worrying about my children, it takes my mind off a life without meaning or purpose. Several years ago, both my son and I had back problems, and things seemed to be getting worse. This condition took place over several months. I ordered books on how to heal the back and was very concerned that this could grow into a major problem.

Then my son sent me a book, though he was secretive about its contents. The book was written by a medical doctor who was very knowledgeable and who taught other doctors. About a third of the way into the book, he stated that the current epidemic of back problems in the United States was due primarily to people who basically did not have any real back problems but were creating problems subconsciously to avoid the real issues in their lives. The pain was real, due to the way the person was breathing, but in truth, there was nothing wrong with the back. I was livid after reading this. Who did this idiot think he was? I kept reading. Halfway through the book, I knew that what he said was true. I closed the book, never to open it again. I returned to working out at the gym like a maniac and totally ignored my back pain. The pain disappeared and never returned. The same was true for my son. We had simply wanted to escape the real problems and fears in our lives, so we created back pain as a diversion.

Many people are preoccupied with staying busy, but the truth is, you cannot run away from what is in your own head. We obsess over our cell phones and want to stay as preoccupied as possible, so we don't have to think about what is really going on with us. Just below the surface of all of this activity, fear is chasing us. This is not the life God wants for us, but it is a life many have chosen.

The sad truth is that a great number of people are not interested in personal growth and would rather lick their wounds and play the role of the victim. If this is who you are, this book is not for you. Narrow is the gate that leads to life, and those who enter through it are few. Many people on this broken planet spend a lifetime building up treasures, as if they are going to take those treasures with them. In reality, the only thing we take with us is love. The kingdom of the one true God is not of this world, and what we choose in this life is preparing us for the next. I will submit for your consideration that this journey toward love and life is not a journey for cowards. Faith is involved, and courage and faith are one and the same. We will not find freedom or be delivered from our fears without courage. Courage does not mean the absence of fear. On the contrary, courage exists only when fear is present. In the presence of raw fear, trusting in the unconditional love of God is the most difficult thing we will ever do. The reason this is true is because there is no other place or person on earth where one can find this kind of love. God's love is perfect love, and it casts out fear. When you find this love, you have found God.

4

Knowing the Voice of God

Truly knowing God and His voice is an essential key to personal freedom. There are many voices that bombard us, and evil often appears as an angel of light. No one can fully explain to another person what knowing the voice of God means for him or her. We ourselves have to learn to discern His voice. However, I have had people say to me on numerous occasions that God spoke to them, and I knew for certain that what they heard or understood was not from God. If God speaks to you, it will be a voice of love and truth. His voice is patient and kind. His voice is the voice of reconciliation. His voice will be full of hope and life. His voice will be for you a gentle place of shelter. His voice will never violate you in any way imaginable. He will not guilt you or cause you harm. You will never have to prove yourself worthy in any way by having to perform for Him to gain His acceptance. He wants the very best for you. If you make a bad decision in your life, He will wait for you until you change your mind. He will not force you or threaten you to change. He will never enable or empower you to do anything destructive. He is a God of life and love. God is light and goodness, and there is no darkness in Him.

On many occasions in my life, God has spoken to me specifically in words that I clearly understood in plain English. Sometimes God communicates with me in a way that transcends language. It's a sense of knowing in my spirit that I cannot explain or put into words. When I find myself getting short and angry with those around me, I often ask to be delivered from myself. In those moments, He just changes my attitude, based on my request, without words. When it comes to issues of forgiveness, or if I am having a problem with another person and that individual agrees to pray with me, there has never been a time when He hasn't shown up to answer us. Not once! He always shows up and delivers us.

Previously, I felt empty in a very important relationship in my life. The other person felt the same way. We each viewed the other as self-absorbed. It was crystal clear to each of us just how flawed and self-centered the other one was. We recognized that each of us had our own individual faults, but we both were convinced that the relationship was on the ropes because of the other person. Completely defeated, I asked this person whether she wanted to pray, and she said yes. I started talking to the Lord, and after a few moments, I became aware that a stronghold existed between us. I told the woman about the stronghold and was astonished when she agreed. We asked the Lord to break the stronghold, and it was immediately broken. In one moment, the relationship was completely restored. Neither of us had a clue as to the nature of the stronghold. Actually, I wasn't even sure what a stronghold was at that time; I just knew we had been delivered from one. Strongholds will be discussed later.

If you find it difficult to ask God to intervene when

problems exist in your relationships, it's only because you have never tried it, or it is an issue of pride. There has never been a time in my life when a person agreed to pray with me that God hasn't shown up and delivered us. He always comes through. There have been a few times when family or friends have refused to pray with me and didn't want reconciliation. We remain estranged to this day.

When I say God always shows up, that doesn't mean He always says things I want to hear. One morning while I was fishing, I was talking to the Lord about another friend of mine. I was upset with the Lord that He hadn't answered this person's prayers, and I was speaking to Him in a dogmatic and aggressive manner. Right in the middle of the conversation, the Lord said to me, "I don't want you talking to Me this way. I have laid a basis in your life for you to trust Me." Well, that stopped me in my tracks. I said, in a much quieter and gentler tone, "I know that is true, but I care about this woman." And the Lord fired back at me, "I care and love this woman far more than you do." I mean, what could I say? I thought for a minute and was speechless.

And that wasn't the worst of it. Several years ago, I had a fight with a friend over loaning my automobile to her sister. I just didn't want to loan her sister my car. I can be very possessive when it comes to my things. This issue of being possessive grew between us to the point that I thought it could cost me our relationship. She came from a family that was very generous and shared everything. My family was just the opposite. We did, however, decide to pray about this, so I turned it over to the Lord. But frankly, I admit, I felt a bit smug, knowing the Lord would not make me loan my car to her sister. After all, it was my choice. Late that same day, I fell asleep. At two o'clock in the morning, the Lord woke me up and spoke specifically to me about this issue. He said to me, "This is the same de-monic spirit that controlled your Dad." That is all He said. Yet the illumination that went through my spirit enlightened those words a thousand-fold. The Lord was not angry with me, nor was He upset. He spoke kindly to me and was very matter-of-fact. He was simply answering my prayer, and I knew what He was saying was absolutely true. I had been blinded to the truth. I was very upset with this revelation, and I couldn't believe that I was being influenced and had bought into this demonic spirit. Needless to say, I apologized several times to my friend and willingly loaned her sister my car.

I'm not saying there is a formula here in what I'm writing, but I can promise you this: if you want to communicate with God, He does hear you, and He will answer you.

If a person were to ask me about my relationship with God, I would say that He is my best friend, but really, He is more like a Father. Most earthly fathers are so unlike God that some people may react badly to that statement. Real Fathers want the very best for their children, in love, and that is Who God is. For certain, we should realize one thing about God when communicating with Him: He is not like Santa Claus. God is not into bargaining at all. God is not into granting wishes on a wish list, nor does He deliver me from my circumstances. He is definitely not going to change other people for our own benefit.

Most of us want to be delivered from the Goliaths in our lives, as we plead with God to make the giants go away. Well, God is not going to make the giant disappear. He will take away your fear of Goliath, so you can face him. We all walk through the valley of the shadow of death. There are times when letting go of the old, in order to make room for the new, is painful—as painful as any physical pain. For example, most of us think of depression as a bad thing, when often it is part of our growth process. In order to grow, one has to give up the "old part of the self," before being able to move into newness. Depression is often an indicator pointing to our need to let go of the old, in order to discover the new. About five years ago, I experienced a very difficult period in my life. I was facing a divorce that I didn't want to go through. There were times when I suffered bouts of depression. These experiences were as if fog or darkness had settled over my soul. I didn't know where the depression was coming from. I felt as if a drug had been injected into me, draining me of all joy and hope.

The first thing the Holy Spirit revealed to me was that I was not being punished; I was being shown that things simply could no longer be "the way they used to be." I had to leave the old, before ever finding the new. So I asked myself a question: "What is causing my depression that I must give up?" I took a pen and paper and started writing a list. The list included a lot of material things that I truly valued. In the same vein, my sense of self-worth, based on material success, was on the line. I thought I would look bad in the eyes of other people, because failure was involved. I had to give up feelings of security, because change would be necessary. The list grew. I looked at the list when I was finished, and I knew that all things to be given up were temporal in nature. That knowledge did not make giving up items on the list any easier, so I turned those items over to the Lord. Minutes later, the depression was gone and did not return.

I don't want to make this process sound simplistic. The depression was gone and did not return, but working through the grief took time. During the last five years, since my divorce, the Lord has taught me more about loving my former wife than I knew when I was married to her. He has given me the eyes to see her through His eyes. Learning to really love her after a bitter and difficult divorce has set me free. Of course, what I am writing about is absolutely impossible unless it's fueled by the power of a loving God, Who can change the old into something completely new. I have not spoken one word to my former wife but have communicated to her on several occasions through emails that I have a desire to pray with her. My desire is bringing peace and forgiveness. Her refusal to meet with me has had no bearing on my growth or freedom. It is God Who heals us and gives us the capacity to love. It is God's love that sets us free.

If you have never really communicated with God, in the way I'm suggesting, this may seem a little strange to you, but, believe me, it's not. All you have to do is learn for yourself. I will give you some suggestions that I have found helpful. First, you will never be able to manipulate God in any way possible. God is God, and we are not. Second, there will be times when He answers you immediately, and there will be times that He won't. I have repeatedly asked God certain questions that I wanted answers for, and in one case, it was more than a year before He answered me. There have been times when, out of nowhere, He has spoken to me. Third, and most important, I'm absolutely positive that I'm not a special person or a righteous man, in and of myself. Whoever you are, as you read this, there is a very good chance that you are a far better person that I am. Most people who really know me will agree with this. If you are not a better person, it doesn't matter one bit. God will communicate with you, if that is what you want. He wants that relationship with all of us.

We were created to be connected to God in love and to be intimate with Him and to communicate with Him, but why do so few people really hear and know His voice? The answer is very simple. It is fear. We are afraid of God. We fear God, because we don't know Who He is. We think God is a god of rules and laws and will punish us. He is not that god! He is a God of love.

Every culture and every person at some point comes under the bondage of law. Laws exist because we live in a world that lacks love. If you love your neighbor, you will not kill him. If you love your neighbor, you won't cheat him or steal from him. If you love your neighbor, you won't lie to him. If you love your neighbor, you won't drive drunk, speeding through a school zone at sixty miles an hour. You won't rape your neighbor, and you won't be a terrorist who blows people up because they believe differently about God than you do.

Good laws are necessary in any culture because they help protect individuals from the lack of love and the evil things people do. The principle of law is necessary, and the authority behind law is punishment. The fear of punishment keeps people from breaking the law. Law is a necessary part of the evolutionary process, but law will never bring us to life. How could law bring us to life? The entire basis for keeping the law is the avoidance of punishment, and the motivation is based on fear. And there is no fear in love, because perfect love casts out fear. In Christ, all death and fear of punishment has been swallowed up, and now, by the power of the indwelling Holy Spirit, we can love. This love gives us the power to overcome fear. When we communicate with God, we have nothing to fear, because God is love.

I cannot emphasize enough that the safest place we can be is in our relationship with God. We don't have to hide from Him. We can tell Him our darkest secrets, and He will not harm us. As we look back over our lives, there are actions we have taken, things we have thought and haven't done that we need forgiveness for. If you have accepted the finished work of Christ, you are forgiven. Period! If you haven't accepted that gift, do it now; it won't take you more than a minute. Say, "Jesus, thank you for dying for me, so I can live eternally in love with You."

There are certainly times when I still blow it, and I willingly admit to God that I have failed, but I don't live with any sense of guilt, because I know God doesn't guilt us. There are areas in my life that I wish I could change, and I talk to the Lord about those areas. Sometimes those changes are slow in coming; real change takes place only as we are transformed by love. Fear never heals anything and only exacerbates the problem.

I first learned that fear heals nothing many years ago. When I was in my thirties, I had violent dreams almost every night. I really had no clue why I was having those dreams. I was married at the time, and I had three children. During this period, I became friends with a Catholic priest, which was very unusual because I had no affiliation with the Catholic Church. The man was a gentle, kind person, and I felt free to talk to him about who I really was, without feeling that he would condemn me. I didn't feel as if I needed to hide from him. I could confess my failures and mistakes to him without receiving his judgment, something that was new for me. As our friendship grew, one day he made a confession to me. My new friend was a homosexual. Until that time in my life, I had been afraid of homosexuals and didn't want to be around them. My religious upbringing had clearly damned all such people. All of that disappeared from my life with my new friend.

I looked within myself without fear. Could I be a homosexual? I determined at the time that if I were a homosexual, I would be one. But I wasn't. My friend was, and it was perfectly all right with me that he was, and I could love him, even though I am not. And guess what happened to me? My violent dreams disappeared. Gone! So were my fear and condemnation of people whose inclinations are different than mine. As I have stated, this experience was when I first discovered that healing takes place only in love. It would be many years after this, however, before I discovered that all healing takes place in love—in love without fear of condemnation or judgment.

All of us are bent and flawed in one way or another. Love covers a multitude of sins. Law never works, because the law has no power to change us. I am absolutely honest and open with God, and I am very aware that He knows everything about me. Even the hairs on my head are numbered. When we try to hide from God, we are only fooling ourselves. The only reason we hide from Him is because we don't know Who He is. I don't cower before God because I don't need to.

A few weeks ago, I caught the flu, and, for reasons unknown to me, I became very angry with God. I really vented my feelings and felt like Jonah; I was ready to get on a ship and flee to another country. It was confusing to me at the time, because I had not been angry with God for a very long time. The following day I sorted things out, and the picture came into perspective. The problem was in me. God didn't become angry or upset with me for being angry with Him. He knew all along what I was wrestling with, and He waited for me to come to Him. We can be who we are before God without fear.

Each person has to work this out for himself or herself, but we have to be real. God is not interested in "let's pretend" or meaningless rituals. What kind of god would delight in or require us to live with meaningless rituals? The God I know and love wants us to be real and honest with Him. In fact, He is the One we can completely trust.

5

The Voice of Evil

Satan and demonic forces exist, whether we believe in them or not. When I first arrived on Kauai on that fateful "business trip" in 1987, I did not believe in Satan or demons. On that trip, I discovered how completely wrong I was. Pretending evil forces do not exist has no benefit. Not being aware of evil has no benefit. Being controlled by evil, unknowingly, brings about death, just as surely as knowingly submitting to evil.

When many people think of Satan and demons, ghoulish figures often come to mind. Historically, we picture gargoyles or little red men running around, holding pitchforks, which has little to do with reality. The most seductive form of evil in my life presented itself as an angel of light; namely, the pretense of good disguising evil. Satan has primarily two ways in which he (or it) buys our allegiance. He either tries to seduce us, or, if that doesn't work, he uses fear. Satan is after power and control, and he wants our worship. Satan is consumed with itself. The demonic world is completely devoid of and incapable of love. The demonic world knows nothing of forgiveness. The world of evil, as it relates to human beings, is really about self-absorption. Satan will offer you the world, if that's what it takes to seduce you. Many people who have risen to power, fame, and wealth have made pacts with the evil one, knowingly or unknowingly. When Christ walked this earth, Satan promised Him all of the kingdoms of this world, if Jesus would fall down and worship him. Without hesitation, Jesus told him to get lost, because His kingdom is not of this world.

The voice of Satan can be very enticing, and that voice can make us feel very sure and right about ourselves, but there will be no love in that voice. The fruit of the Spirit is evident when we see Who God is. That fruit is love, joy, peace, patience, kindness, goodness, faithfulness, gentleness, and self-control. Not so with the seduction of Satan; there may be visions of grandeur and the hope of pleasures without end, but the final result is death. Everything that proceeds out of the mouth of Satan is a lie. He is a liar, and there is no truth or love in him.

Before we look at how Satan comes at us, it is important to understand who he is: the essence of its spirit. Satan is known as the accuser. The very Greek word for Satan means "the accuser," "the hater." If one characteristic leaps out to explain who Satan is, it is found in the spirit of judgment. In its nature, a judgmental spirit assumes the "moral high ground" and affords us a feeling of superiority over those whom we are judging. There is power in this thinking that renders us justified and right in our own minds. It helps us establish a false sense of authority, control, and well-being. Nowhere in this spirit is there love or forgiveness. The spirit of judgment allows us to feel better about ourselves, at the expense of others.

This spirit of judgment I am writing about takes the authority that belongs solely to God. God and God alone has the capacity to judge us, and in love that judgment is found in the finished work of Jesus Christ. Jesus died for you and me, so we could share His life in love forever.

All of us, at one time or another, have judged someone wrongly. This evil spirit I am writing about doesn't avoid showing itself to those closest to us. As a matter of fact, this spirit often rears its ugly head with those we know best. It's very important that we are able to discern various spirits, because there is no doubt that a spirit of discernment exists when love needs to be protected by boundaries. (We will discuss boundaries later.) For now, I am addressing the spirit that characterizes the very nature of evil, and that spirit is one of pride. Pride, at its core, becomes its own god and is incapable of love. This spirit sets itself above another and feeds off the energy and attitude of superiority. This is the very mind-set of Satan.

Satan approaches us in a multitude of ways and communicates using different voices. Sometimes he approaches us directly, and other times he speaks to us through people. Appealing to our egos is as old to Satan as human history. In the Garden of Eden, Satan promised Adam and Eve that they would become just like God and find the keys to the Kingdom, independent of, and separated from, the God Who loved them. Satan promises us the same, with seemingly endless possibilities devoid of love but with the promise of happiness. "If I were rich or won the lottery, I would be happy." "If could just find the perfect mate to marry, I would be happy." "If I just had that job or belonged to this club or owned that new house or looked like that person, then I would be happy." The list of our wants and desires is staggering, as we try to find meaning and life separated from the God Who loves us. Satan will point us in any direction, as long as it is not connected to God.

If Satan cannot seduce us with a myriad of possibilities for finding happiness, he will attack us with fear. All of the fear in our lives is directly or indirectly related to Satan. When Adam and Eve ate from the forbidden fruit and chose to find meaning and life separated from God, fear was born. The first words out of Adam's mouth, after feeling fear, were "I was afraid." Adam hid from God and tried to cover himself with fig leaves, and, separated from the love of God, we still do the same today.

One of Satan's favorite tactics is to come at us using flaming darts. A thought will come to mind, and that thought seems to originate from our own inner selves. These thoughts could be ugly or lewd, or they could be vague feelings, as if some threat or pending doom awaits us or someone we love. These darts may be irrational in nature, and the more we try to reason them away, the more powerful they become. There is a foreboding energy behind these thoughts and feelings. Sometimes these thoughts and fears suddenly come upon us at the strangest times. One minute we can feel absolutely sure and confident and the next moment feel all alone, overcome by feelings of dread.

Millions of people suffer from various obsessive-compulsive disorders, ranging from mild to severe, but they all have their origin in fear. Psychologists have named many of these disorders, but there is a malevolent spirit behind these names and conditions. Trying to explain all of these flaming darts in scientific, humanistic terms may be helpful, but knowledge alone lacks the ability to free and heal us.

Recently, a person I know was going to a well-known psychologist for counseling. The psychologist was highly recommended by another PhD who counsels in drug addiction. In the middle of this individual's therapy, the psychologist took his own life, leaving behind a wife and two children. He left no note! He just wanted out of this world. Here was a man who could define the problems of life with the precision of a surgeon but had no power to heal. He could not even heal himself. None of us can. It is the love of God that transforms us. I am not talking about nice little ideas here, such as "Let's just think good thoughts." I am writing about an enemy who roars around like a raging lion, seeking someone to devour! There are millions of people held captive by Satan through fear. The good news is that in Christ, evil is completely defeated. Satan has no authority over us whatsoever. He comes at us with lies and distortions, threatening with all kinds of evil promises that are as empty as he is. We simply have to learn who we are in Christ and discover for ourselves the fact that we are victorious.

6

Faith and Courage

When writing about faith or courage, I do not mean mustering up the willpower to sacrifice ourselves to a god who, in fact, is no god at all.

Take a good look at those young men who flew the planes into the World Trade Center on 9/11/2001. Those young men were willing to give up their lives because they were convinced that Americans were the enemy. Talk about faith and courage, these men had it. They believed that what they were doing was for God. Righteous indignation burned within them, and they sacrificed their lives to an angry god whom they worshipped. Yet all of their faith and sacrifice was in vain. It didn't matter how much they "believed." The object of their faith was based in a lie.

The focus of real faith is never about us. Our old nature will often say, "I gotta believe, I gotta believe, I gotta believe." Someone with this kind of faith thinks, "The reason God didn't come through for me was that I didn't believe hard enough." This type of thinking is total horseshit and has nothing to do with real faith. Real faith means depending on and trusting the

Lord, Who loves us. We can trust that God will be there for us, and He will give us the faith we need to face whatever comes into our lives. Peter, one of Jesus's disciples, boldly declared to Jesus that he would never deny Him. Before the night was over, out of fear, Peter had denied Jesus three times. At the end of his life, Peter chose to be crucified upside down without fear, and you can bet your life that Jesus was right there with him, and His grace was sufficient. The faith that I am writing about comes from God and is part of our transformation from the old to the new.

Looking back over my life, I see that certain fears often plagued me when it came to trusting God. One of those areas, in particular, concerned my finances. I'm not a trusting person. I am very aware of how flawed all of us are. Figuring out exactly when I should trust God and when something is my responsibility has not been easy. My philosophy about money has been to work my butt off, live within my means, and put money in the bank. Several years ago, when I was in the middle of building my business, I was involved in a situation where I felt that an individual had cheated me out of a considerable amount of money. He was within the letter of the law, so I really couldn't sue him. In essence, he took the work I had done and turned the business over to one of his cronies. I'd done the work; the other guy was paid. I was livid—not only was I angry, I just couldn't let it go. A friend told me that I just needed to trust God and get on with my life. That statement only added fuel to the fire.

"You trust God," I retorted to this person, in a very unfriendly tone of voice.

Several days passed, but I kept wrestling with this issue. One night, about three o'clock in the morning, I got out of bed and went into another room. I couldn't stop obsessing over this situation. Finally, I turned to the Lord in a state of complete frustration and asked, "What do You want from me?" I was half yelling and said it again, "What do You want from me?"

Just as clear as a bell, the Lord spoke to me: "I want you to trust Me."

The next words out of my mouth were, "I do trust You." A moment later, I felt complete peace fall over me. The issue was settled, and I never gave it another thought.

In religion, faith is dependent on what I do. In religion, faith is dependent on my sacrifice. I have actually heard grown men say from their pulpits, when passing the collection plate, that God needs our money. What kind of a god would need my money? That has to be one pathetic god, if he needs my money. The God I know needs nothing from me. The God I know wants to give me His life. He wants me to trust Him, so I can grow in love. The God I know wants me to be generous with my money because of delight in sharing what I have with others. This is the kind of faith that comes from God working in my life. This is the kind of faith that is in response to love.

I'm not trying to make this sound easy, because it's not. One morning, soon after I was married to a woman with considerable wealth, I got out of bed and fell to the floor with a dizzy spell. This had never happened to me before, and I thought I was having a stroke or something worse. Fear absolutely engulfed me. Nothing, and I mean nothing, could be worse for me than having to be taken care of by the woman I had just married. I was numb with fear. I immediately went to the Lord and asked Him to take away my fear. I told Him I didn't care if I was dying from a brain tumor or whatever this was, I wanted the fear gone. Within minutes, He answered my request, and I was completely at peace. I couldn't see the doctor until the following day, and during that time, I was as calm as I could be. The fear was gone. When I saw the doctor, I discovered that it was an inner ear problem and easily cured. I didn't have to muster up the faith for anything, other than to ask the Lord to take away my fear.

A few years ago, my closest and best friend was killed by a hit-and-run driver. This person had known me better than any human being on earth and had loved me. A couple of years before this happened, I had gone through a difficult divorce that was not my choice. My former wife's grown son had overdosed on heroin and died two days before Christmas. The cracks in our relationship became the Grand Canyon. This period of time was very difficult for me, and just as I was starting to put the pieces of my life back together, my closest friend was killed. Talk about my faith being tested, and yet I knew God was right there with me. I had so many questions without any answers.

Six weeks after my friend died, I was allowed to speak to him in the middle of the night. This was not a dream. My friend was about thirty-five years old when I spoke to him in the vision, but he had been sixty-six when he was killed. The love that I felt for him when he appeared to me had such overwhelming power that I still often think of it. We spoke briefly, and then he was gone. I had not asked for this experience to happen, but the Lord knew that I needed it. Though I dearly miss my friend and cannot wait to meet him again, I have never wanted him back on earth with me, because to want this would be very selfish on my part. So it is with all of those we love who have gone before us. We can trust them with the God of Glory.

Some people may find it difficult to believe what I'm saying, and perhaps others simply cannot believe or trust in God at all. I completely identify with those of you who feel this way. For so many years in my life, I tried to perform for a god who was not really a God. There were many years when I believed in nothing much at all. Yet the God I am writing about does exist, the God I am writing about loves you, and He is just waiting for you to come to Him.

Many years ago I was stuck in that never–never land where I didn't know what I believed. I felt a need to communicate with God but really didn't know what to do. At the time, I was living with a woman who felt much the same way I did. One Sunday morning, I asked her if she wanted to listen to some music and pray with me. She agreed. I put on a tape that I had purchased by Eric Solar, who performed an instrumental titled "Unconditional Love." Something about his music touched my soul. I turned on the tape, became comfortable on the couch, and let the music wash over me. I really didn't know what to pray, so I prayed silently. I placed my hand on my friend's shoulder, and when I did, I felt an energy of pure peace flow through me. I became aware that the Holy Spirit had fallen over her. I did not move or say anything. Soon I noticed tears streaming down her face. At first, I found this to be confusing, because there is no fear when communing with the Holy Spirit. All I could do was wait.

After a period of time, she revealed what had transpired. In those brief moments, my friend saw herself as a lamb held in the arms of the Shepherd. She was being cradled in the lap of God. With certainty, she knew she was completely loved. She was loved simply for who she was—loved for just being. When she felt the tears spilling down her cheeks, she wanted to stop them and said so to the Shepherd. It was then that she realized the tears were not her own. The tears streaming down her eyes came from the Lord. They were God's tears. God felt her pain. He infinitely felt her pain more than she did. God was crying for her.

This is Who God is, yet it can be a scary thing to surrender your mind and heart to the living God, because you have to establish this relationship for yourself. Getting naked before Him is not all that easy. There are no fig leaves—there's nothing to hide behind, no one to hold your hand. The preacher or the priest won't be there. Neither will Mom or Dad, brother or sister, husband or wife, friend or support group—no one will be there but you and Him. It is so difficult for us to be completely honest with God, because we don't know Him. For most of our lives, we have been fed nothing but lies about Who God is. Many people are giving lip service to a god who is not God at all.

If I were to ask you to name what you think are some of the most difficult things to do, you would probably have a good list. We could both agree that losing a hundred pounds is tough; so is taking a really big risk, such as quitting an unfulfilling job or leaving a bad marriage. The list could go on and on.

I submit to you that one of the hardest things in the world is for us to fully and truly comprehend how much God loves us. We say we know that God loves us, but everything about us screams that we really don't know this at all. If we are completely honest with ourselves, our "knowing" this isn't pure or complete. It is sometimes clouded by doubts, especially when we think we have failed. It is obscured, because we feel unworthy for no good reason, other than the fact that, as one of my friends says, "It just cannot be that easy." Many times, it really is more of a hope that God loves us, rather than assured, ironclad, absolute certainty that God does love us, no matter what. We don't have any other examples of this type of love anywhere in our human experience.

I cannot do this for you. No one can. The choice to bring

the God of love into our lives is not easy. Pride gives us a terrible fight. Just remember, it is not our job to change our perception but to invite the Holy Spirit to change us. Yet we have to take the leap into His arms.

7

Spiritual Warfare

The Apostle Paul was one of the most religious men of his day, until he met Jesus while walking on the road to Damascus. After Paul's meeting with Jesus, his world was turned upside down. Paul thought he was doing God's work by persecuting and killing Christians. After this encounter, his life, as he knew it, came to an end. Paul knew a great deal about spiritual warfare, because he had been trapped in religion. Near the end of his life, after working through so many strongholds, Paul wrote this about his life: "I have fought the good fight; I have finished the race; I have kept the faith." Not a bad epitaph for anyone who is interested in growing in love.

Earlier in this book, I wrote about being delivered from a stronghold, and at that time, I didn't really know what a stronghold was. I now understand the nature of a stronghold. When a person (or persons) is in a stronghold, the power of that stronghold lies in the fact that the individual cannot see that he or she is caught. The power is in the lie. A stronghold is when we are being influenced by a satanic spirit of death, but, at the same time, we cannot see it. At such times, we can clearly see the speck in our brother's eye but fail to see the log in our own eye. This is especially true for those trapped in religion.

God delivered me from a stronghold, but it was more than a year before He would tell me the specifics of what that was. The stronghold existed between my wife and me. The Lord said, "The stronghold is this. You each felt that the stronghold was in the other person." My interpretation of His words was that we were both prideful and caught in a spirit of judgment, each blaming the other.

Strongholds are particularly common among people with a religious mind-set. Religion has always been the enemy of God. When I speak of religion, I am not writing about spiritual growth or growing in love, as some people use this word. I am talking about a return to bondage. Religion is man's way of trying to find God, based on his own performance. The truth of the matter is, because we ourselves are angry and punishing, we have created that idea about God. We have created God in our own image. That is the core of religion.

In reality, God created us in His image, which is love. It is God Who came to us in the person of Christ. It is God Who died for you and me so that we could live. In religion, we have god killing the infidels because of a spirit of moral superiority. In religion, we try to appease this god with money and sacrifices, so that he will be good to us and not punish us. All religions are basically the same at their core. I don't care if we are talking about Muslim extremists blowing people up or apostate Christianity. Religion is the enemy of God. The God I know wants a relationship with us, and that relationship is based in love. We do not have to hide from Him, nor do I have to perform for Him. He loves and accepts me right where I am, with all of my flaws and shortcomings. His goal for me is to grow in love, and the way He accomplishes that goal is by loving me.

I can place myself in God's care and be sure I am in the safest place I can possibly be. That is not true of religion.

The religious people of Jesus's day hated Him. Jesus openly rebuked them and said, "How can you speak good when you are evil?" When you think about it, to a bystander, this must have been very confusing. Jesus was hanging out with all types of people who were outcasts in His culture. Not only did He hang out with these people, He performed numerous miracles for them and then made them His disciples. At the same time, He strongly rebuked the people who were revered as the "spiritual leaders" of that day. How could this be? How could He call those dedicated religious people evil?

Let me put the question this way: "What is the difference between a person who is flawed and makes many mistakes, which includes all of us, and one who is evil?" An evil person is one who has crossed over the line and is characterized by a refusal to tolerate the sense of his or her own sinfulness. Man, separated from God and, under the law, will feel guilt. The reason that we feel guilt is that we cannot keep the law. The lie of Satan is just that. It is a lie. You cannot be like God, knowing good and evil. Fear and guilt under the law are good things. Can you imagine living in a country without laws? Overnight, men would become like animals. Not being under the law and without guilt or restraint, you have Ted Bundy, Hitler, and millions of others in the world who have committed untold atrocities by being given over to evil. It doesn't take much discernment to come to the conclusion that serial killers and child molesters are seriously flawed.

It is easy to see that these people have crossed over a line into death, but what about the religious? How could Jesus call these people evil? Good and evil, in reality, are connected to a Spirit of good or a spirit of evil. Good is connected to God and

His Spirit, and His Spirit is connected to life and liveliness. In this Spirit, we have love, joy, peace, and a host of other attributes that make life good. These attributes are good, because they are connected to the Creator God. Satan has been evil and a liar and a murderer from the beginning. Satan creates nothing but illusion and death. Satan kills life and liveliness, and the "good" that Satan promised is a lie. When speaking of what it means to be a Christian, Saint Therese of Lisieux said, "If you are willing to serenely bear the trial of being displeasing to yourself, then you will be for Jesus, a pleasant place of shelter." Not only did the religious people not bear the trial of being displeasing to themselves when confronted with the Messiah, the very One they were promised, they killed Him. This is the spirit of Satan.

It is not uncommon in religion for people to sacrifice others to preserve their own self-image of perfection. We see this all of the time in our country. I have witnessed many people, in the name of god, picking on homosexuals, Muslims, and a hoard of other sinners to whom they feel morally superior and condemning sins they deem inappropriate. Psychologists call this "scapegoating." These people sacrifice others to preserve their own self-image. Deep down, evil people feel themselves to be faultless, but, sooner or later, they find themselves in conflict with others. Invariably, they perceive the conflict to be the other person's fault. Because they must deny their own sin, they must perceive others as sinful. Evil people never think of themselves as evil, and this is the stronghold.

In Jesus's time, look at how utterly dedicated the religious were to preserving their own self-image of perfection. One person said of Jesus, "He casts out demons by the prince of demons." These same people unceasingly engaged in an effort to maintain the appearance of moral purity. Most people are very aware of, and sensitive to, social norms and what others might think about them. Their "goodness" is all on a level of pretense. This pretense is at the core of who Satan is, and it is the lie. This is the spirit that crucified Christ. It was into this world that Jesus came, and He came for us. He came to give us His life, and He knew it would cost Him His own. Jesus knew that it was impossible to change our old nature. He came so that we could live to be totally free from the bondage of guilt and law.

The only way I know to break a stronghold is through love. Of course, the difficulty lies in seeing that we are caught in a stronghold. I have discovered that when I think I'm right and that right becomes bigger than love, there is a good chance I'm caught in a stronghold. Love covers a multitude of sins.

I mentioned earlier that my best friend for more than forty years had been killed. He is my ultimate illustration of what love is all about when it comes to another person. When two people come together in the love of God, as we did, the walls that appear to separate them completely disappear. That was true of Jim and me. From a human-interest standpoint, we had nothing in common. Nothing! Jim was a hippie in the sixties, and he never really changed. He was a wild-looking man who rode Harley motorcycles and was still getting tattoos at age sixty-five. He looked like John the Baptist, with long hair and a full beard, and he could be very reclusive. We didn't like the same movies or music, and we never socialized just to socialize. I didn't care for his humor, nor he, mine. We had nothing in common, except the love of Christ, and that love transcended everything. Here is the really important part, and I want you to understand this. I often told Jim that he was "the most despicable person I knew and the only person on earth I felt morally superior to." He would just laugh at me and fire back, "It's my gift." We saw each other's flaws and imperfections with amazing clarity, yet they held no meaning or power for either of us. None, whatsoever! We loved each other with the Spirit of Christ. We could talk for hours on end, being totally ourselves, with no sense of judgment, and never miss a beat. You have no idea how much I miss him.

If you are caught in a stronghold, you will have a great deal of fear in your life, no matter how much you are living with denial. All pretense is connected to a lie, and the only reason we lie is because we are afraid. First, we have the fear of exposure: "What if people find out who I really am?" I appear one way to the world, but, on the inside, I know who I am. We are afraid, so we lie. The truth is, we have no reason to lie. God knows everything about us, and He loves us unconditionally. In Christ, all of our mistakes, sins, and shortcomings have been forgiven. To the religious people of His day, the very people who nailed Him to that cross, Jesus cried out, "Father, forgive them, for they know not what they do."

I also want to mention the nonreligious strongholds that keep millions of people in personal bondage. These are strongholds that are much more noticeable and not as easily hidden. I am writing about our addictions. Of course, many of us who are addicted don't view ourselves as being in slavery to our addictions, but we are. Giving up an addiction can seem like an impossibility. If you take my addiction away from me, I will feel completely empty on the inside. Life seems to have no meaning apart from that addiction; just ask any alcoholic, workaholic, sex addict, food addict, or drug addict. There are so many addictions in our culture; the list is staggering. The pain and emptiness point to a lack of wholeness and love. All addictions have their bases in fear. It is certainly true that without Jesus, we can do nothing when it comes to real life and love. It is equally true that in Him, there is nothing that cannot be undone.

A major drawback in handling our addictions at the level of symptoms is that even when "victory" is obtained, without tackling the real underlying issue, which is spiritual death, we are often left constantly struggling against that bondage. I know people who have been on a "diet" for thirty years. In fact, the very word *diet* implies that we are depriving ourselves, holding something back that we really want. This leads to a life of constant struggle and usually relegates us to a roller coaster of "good times" and "bad." The secret to true freedom is to be set free from the cause of our problems and to stop dealing with the symptoms.

8

Transformation from Fear to Love

The core issue we all battle on this broken planet is spiritual death. By spiritual death, I mean we have been separated from the unconditional love of God. When Adam and Eve chose to eat from the tree of the knowledge of good and evil, in essence, they sought to find meaning and purpose separated from the God Who loved them. In love, God warned them not to eat from the tree that represented separation from Him. He warned Adam and Eve that they would die, but Adam and Eve ignored God's warning. They embraced the lie of Satan and determined to find life and meaning separated from love.

Some may ask why God placed that particular tree in the Garden? The answer is very simple: to give us freedom. We are created in the image of God, and that means we have the freedom to choose, unlike the rest of the creation. God does not force us to do anything. The easiest Being to ignore or say no to is the Holy Spirit, because the Holy Spirit always deals with us in love. We can ignore the Spirit's attempt to lead the way, to our own detriment, but the Spirit will not take away our choice. That choice essentially is a choice for love. This is not true of Satan, with its lies and distortions. Satan rules by fear! Satan is the author of bondage and death.

Adam and Eve were created in the Garden of Eden, where love reigned in a world of perfection. They were completely free and naked and not ashamed. It was into this world that Satan came and offered them a choice, and that choice was founded on the lie "You shall be like God." And when they ate from that forbidden tree, they entered into a relationship with Satan and spiritual death. Fear was immediately born, and Adam hid in the Garden and covered himself with fig leaves.

In one very real sense, we are all making our way back to the Garden for which we were created. Adam and Eve were created in a world of perfect love and then made the choice to be like God, independent of love. Now we live in a fallen world of fear and chaos, and we have to make the choice for love. At times, especially in those moments of real pain when all seems lost and hopeless, this may feel completely unfair. After all, that was Adam and Eve's choice, not mine. But eternal questions are being answered here, and each one of us must cast his or her vote. I am saying to you that these slight momentary afflictions are preparing us for an eternal weight of Glory beyond all comparison. I have seen the Glory that awaits us.

Actually, the fall of Adam and Eve in the final analysis is bringing us into a higher state of being. Before Adam and Eve could eat from the Tree of Life, they were driven out of the Garden because of spiritual death. God is a God of life and love, and there is no death in Him. God will not reign or coexist with death. When we leave this broken planet, where Satan resides, and enter the Glory that God has prepared for us, we will never taste of death again. For, you see, Jesus is the Tree of Life and the New Creation. Only God could swallow up death and come out the other side, which He accomplished when He raised Jesus in love. Jesus is the first born of the dead and the Tree of Life. We are a New Creation in Him.

⌒ᘯᕐᘯ⌒

Once I was flying home from a business trip, heading to the Dallas-Fort Worth airport. It was a night flight, and there were empty seats. A flight attendant approached me and asked whether she could have a few minutes of my time. During the next half hour, she told me about an affair she was having with one of the pilots, who was married. She was at a crisis point in her life and needed to make a decision.

"What should I do?" she pleaded.

The pilot in question would not leave his wife. We continued to talk, and I asked her many questions. As our conversation developed, it seemed to me that the pilot also needed to make some decisions. Finally, after more deliberation, I told her that I had an answer for her, and she looked hopefully at me.

"When we get to Dallas," I said, "don't call him."

A sad look fell over her face, and she looked away from me. "I'll do anything but that," she said. "Anything but that."

I cannot tell you the number of times I have heard that statement in my life: "I will do anything but that."

I'm not trying to say that this young woman should have listened to me and taken my advice. I am, however, making the point that this woman was being controlled and motivated by fear. Her desire to be with this pilot was driven by loneliness and need. If you need another person to the point that you cannot live without him or her, you cannot love that person. When you love, you are not preoccupied with just your own desires because love has the capacity to see the other person apart from your own needs. If I truly love someone, I want the best for that person, even if that person doesn't want to be with me.

On one level, we are all needy when it comes to love. Our self-centered nature doesn't want to see that our loneliness doesn't come from not receiving love from others. Our pain stems from the love we ourselves aren't giving to others in the present. And yet we cannot give what we do not possess, if we are empty and lonely. This is a universal problem for all of mankind and the reason we see so little love around us. We have to get our needs met before we can truly love another; however, there is a surrendering process before this can happen. This process is impossible to achieve without the working of the Holy Spirit. It is not our job to change our perception but to invite the Holy Spirit into our lives to change us. People who set out in their own natural strength to love and change the world by loving their neighbors as themselves are going to become bitter, cynical, and disillusioned. We cannot find love and life separated from God.

Fear is overcome through love, but there is no formula for growing in love. Think of all of the self-help books that have been written and the number of people in our culture who make their living by listening to and counseling others. The truth is that no one can determine for another person what truly applies to his or her life and circumstances. Ultimately, it is our own personal connection to the Holy Spirit that guides us and sets us free.

Growing in love is not always easy. It is a birthing process that can be painful. It seems, during times of real growth, that things around us often seem worse. After my divorce, I felt like Rip Van Winkle, as if I had been sleeping for years, and suddenly I woke up. People whom I thought really loved me no longer would have anything to do with me. Betrayal is difficult to understand until it happens to us. At such times, forgiveness seems so far from us. Personal growth can be so painful, because it makes us feel humble to face our own darkness. Most of us associate success with not failing or stumbling or making mistakes. I know that for me, however, when I am successful through my own strength, I tend to go my own way, and I have no need for God. It is through my problems, failures, and weaknesses that I learn to trust the Lord. My own way is very limited and is all about me and my success and, for the most part, is void of love. I must stay in control because to lose control will cause defeat. Yet the Lord wants to bring me into a larger place. He wants to infuse in me a life beyond anything I could dream of, for he knows how limited I am just within myself. In order to be open to all that God has in store for me, I have not found a path of continual success but one of multiple failures. With each new failure, I have found growth, for I have discovered that resurrection to the new comes only through death of the old.

Real change often occurs slowly not because of God, but because of us. We do not want to change. People who have a judgmental spirit like to judge others. One day I was driving with a woman who just could not stop judging an individual for the harm he had caused her. I kept asking this woman why she was doing this. She knew better, and she knew that this spirit of judgment was causing nothing but harm. Finally, she looked at me and said, "It makes me feel better about myself." We all know gossip is wrong, and yet how many people do you know, including ourselves, who like to gossip? We like feeding at the trough that makes us feel superior to our brothers and sisters. How many people love playing the role of the victim?

These people want to blame others for the bad hand they have been dealt in life. Our pride doesn't want us to see the truth about ourselves, and it wages a terrible fight. I know of people for whom forgiveness remains their only path out of hell, but they still refuse to forgive. We are enslaved to the forces of evil when we are in submission to nothing beyond our own will and pride. The idea that we stand alone in the universe is an illusion. We either belong to God, or we belong to Satan. Jesus said it best when He said, "Whoever will save his life shall lose it. And whoever shall lose his life for My sake shall find it."

What I find so ironic in my own life is that everything that kept me in bondage now looks like madness to me, since I have been delivered. Many years ago I was an alcoholic, and it started to become a real problem. I was a high-functioning alcoholic and worked long days, but when evening came, I wanted to drink—lots of drinks. Only when I was drinking did I have a feeling of wellbeing. The thought of facing life without booze wasn't an option I wanted. The entire motive behind my drinking was fear, and the more I drank, the greater the fear. I didn't look like a fearful guy on the outside. I was into the mixed martial arts and spent many hours kickboxing. I was a successful businessman. I liked riding motorcycles and often partied until the wee hours of the morning. I was also pushing down all of my unresolved issues in life, and the liquor helped me maintain the pretense.

If anyone really knew what it was like to walk in my shoes, I surmised, they would certainly understand why I drank. I'd had a rotten childhood and was raised without the love I need-ed. I had been a sergeant in the Marine Corps and became caught up in the Vietnam War. My life consisted of broken relationships and disappointments, but I kept the engine going with bourbon until I hit bottom. The first six months after I gave up drinking, I would look into the mirror each morning and say, "Boy, do I know why I drank." Facing all of the pain in my past seemed overwhelming at times. Today I am as free as a bird when it comes to alcohol. Many of my friends drink, and it doesn't bother me at all. I simply do not want to drink, and I am not tempted. Alcohol was a symptom of something much bigger in my life: fear and lack of love. All of our addictions are basically the same and have their roots in spiritual death.

I value freedom as much as anyone does. At the same time, I hate fear as much as anyone. Ironically, in order to become free, I must face and feel fear, which is painful. To the degree that I refuse to face my fear, I live in bondage. Personal suffering or pain is an inherent part of learning and growth.

Not long ago, I woke up in the middle of the night, and I was overwhelmed by fear. Immediately, I told the Lord that I did not want to run from those fears. I let the fear wash over me, really feeling it. I did not fight or run from it. I asked the Lord to reveal to me the nature of the fear. Then I realized the fear that I was experiencing was already inside me. The fear was being exposed without pretense, because I was not trying to avoid the emotional pain that accompanied it. Sometimes we have fears deeply embedded in our unconscious or subconscious minds and have no idea how they are there. Such fears could have been there since childhood and could still be there many years later when we are adults. Often a person cannot remember the source of his or her fears or the events that caused them. If you are willing to face the pain of confronting your fears, the Holy Spirit is the ultimate therapist. Once you confront those fears, they lose power over you. You will begin to discover freedom that you have never experienced before.

The most important thing to remember when fear suddenly comes over you is that you are not alone. The fact that your fears are coming to the surface to be brought into the light of day and out of the shadows is a sign of healing. God is right there with you, and He knows exactly what you are going through. All of us, at one time or another, have a "bear in the cave" that we need to face. No one really wants to walk into that cave, but if we really want to be free, we have to face the bear. All of the armies of Israel trembled when Goliath came forward at the Valley of Elah and challenged the God of Israel. Every man of valor in Israel and in Israel's army hid in the trenches, but not David. David was just a boy at the time. David declared, "Who is this uncircumcised Philistine, that he should defy the armies of the living God?" David went out and slew the giant. We all have giants in our lives, and the issue becomes, what are we going to do about them? Do we want to be controlled by our fears and hide in the trenches?

Most of us plead with God to make the giants disappear, when in reality God is preparing us to become giant killers! "Though I walk through the Valley of the Shadow of Death, I fear no evil; for thou art with me."

9

Loving Ourselves

We cannot love another person if we don't love ourselves. I believe it might be worth looking at the definition of love that I'm using, in regard to this work, because it is easy to become confused when it comes to loving ourselves. Often, what we call love is not love at all. Love is that healing energy force in our lives that promotes life and growth and freedom from fear. The love I am writing about comes from God, but the way that love works itself out in our lives does not tie us to a god who stands over us with a big stick, watching and judging our every move. There are so many misconceptions about God. I cannot count the number of times I have heard people say that God is in complete control. That statement is absolutely absurd. God has given us free will, and that choice is a real choice. All of the heinous acts of evil committed at the hands of those who are participating in evil have nothing to do with God. Those acts are completely and totally separated from God.

It is true that there is nothing anyone can do to me that can separate me from the love of God. It is also true that God uses all of the things that have happened in my life for my good. The evil things people plan against me in the end will turn out for my growth. I am not a victim, in any sense of the word, but it is ridiculous to say that God is in complete control. Just look around you at all of the chaos and death in the world. God is not involved in any of that, but none of this death and chaos can thwart His purposes. The reason I bring up this issue is that millions of people are held bondage to a monster god who does not exist. Many people are afraid of God because they feel that if they step out of line, God is going to punish them. God doesn't punish anyone. Ever! The ultimate punishment is when God gives a person over to his or her own desires and choices, separated from love. Hell is the state of being we fashion for ourselves: a state of final separation from God, which is not the result of God's rejection of man, but of man's rejection of God, Who is love.

The energy force of love in our own lives will provide an attitude of acceptance of ourselves, in regard to where we are right now in our own process. That acceptance includes all of our flaws and imperfections. If I cannot love myself where I am today, I do not understand the love that God has for me. This is a choice. I must accept the love that God has for me, and that choice is found in the finished work of Jesus Christ.

The narcissistic personality is looking for perfection, separated from love, which is a way of making sure that love never has a chance to grow. Pride defends against love, but not against fear. Our perceptions of ourselves often become the battleground between pride's desire to judge and love's desire to accept ourselves as we are. The reason we fail to accept ourselves in the moment is because we feel it is our responsibility to be like God, but in truth, it is not. Our responsibility is to be open to what God wants and is doing in us, because He is taking us to a higher place. He does this through a relationship of love.

One way we have of loving ourselves is through boundaries. There is a great deal of information available today concerning boundaries, and one of the best books I have ever read on the subject was written by John Townsend and Henry Cloud. The title of this work is *Boundaries—When to Say Yes and When to Say No*. Boundaries are a way of protecting ourselves when we don't know very much about loving ourselves. The truth is, there have been so many lies perpetuated about what it means to be in a relationship with God, and there are people simply frozen in relationships that have nothing to do with God. Millions of people are stuck in relationships without love, and they believe that is what god wants for them. God doesn't want us stuck in anything.

A very close and dear friend of mine at age twenty-five married a good-looking, charming, and very persistent man. Soon after the marriage, she gave birth to two beautiful twin girls. Over the years, the relationship grew to be destructive. Her husband became more and more dependent on alcohol and drugs and grew physically and psychologically abusive. He often threatened that he would kill her and the children if she ever left him. When she sought counseling, the counselor told her that God did not allow divorce. He reminded her of her two beautiful children and the ten years invested in the marriage. Divorcing her husband would destroy the family unit. My friend took his advice and tried to make the marriage work. She soon became physically ill and almost had a nervous breakdown. Finally, after much struggling, she called it quits and got the divorce. In time, she remarried and enjoyed a beautiful and loving relationship with her second husband that lasted until his death twenty-five years later. When I asked her what had happened to her first husband, she told me that he had committed suicide after his third marriage.

My friend could have benefited from the *Boundaries* book I suggested when she knew very little about loving herself. I personally have some serious questions for the counselor who told her God did not allow divorce. Who in the hell did he think he was? Who could be arrogant enough in the name of God to speak for the Holy Spirit without love?

Boundaries are very important when people don't really understand much about what it means to love themselves. There are so many people who have substituted a life of sacrifice for love that they have lost their way. For those of us who do understand boundaries, what it means to love oneself really becomes more about moving beyond boundaries.

I'm not aware of anything in my life that I would choose to do if someone tried to force me to act against my choice out of fear. The person could put a gun to my head and cock the hammer, but I would not submit. I am not submitting to fear, and that is my choice because I know God loves me, and I love myself. My battles in loving myself originate from a different place. For those of us who know God loves us and have spent a considerable amount of time on this broken planet, we look forward to the day when we can shed these bodies of death for new ones. I can so identify with the apostle Paul when he penned a letter to the church in Rome and wrote, "Wretched man that I am! Who will deliver me from this body of death?"

I have also noticed that when I am with people who do not know the Lord, many are terrified of death and want to live forever. A Hollywood movie producer and a good friend of my brother told him that scientists are researching ways to keep mankind alive until we are 150 years old—maybe, in time, even 1,000 years old. When I think about having to remain on this planet for 150 years, it would feel like being consigned to Hell.

In my own life, what I find difficult is being patient with myself, in regard to the growth process. I have a great appetite for life. I love life. I like to dance, and I love music. I love to fish, and I love the beauty of the Creation. I love laughter, and it is so wonderful when all seems well with the people I know and love. At the same time, I find that the more conscious I become and the more I grow, the more aware I am of how much I really don't belong in the world. I was created for so much more than what exists on this broken planet. The Glory of love that we all seek and that one day will be ours is in direct opposition to the world of fear in which we reside. For those of us who tend to be perfectionists, the process of learning to love ourselves requires becoming more patient with our growth. God will not love us any more in ten million years than He does at this moment.

10

Suffering

Can you imagine what it must have been like for the disciples and Jesus's followers when word spread that he had been taken captive from the Garden of Gethsemane? Many of these people had been with Him during His entire ministry. They had been there when Jesus turned water into wine. They had witnessed Jesus feeding the multitudes with a few fish and a few loaves of bread. Some were there when he walked on water. He had healed the sick and made the blind able to see. He cast out demons and raised the dead. He spoke with authority, and His words had pierced their hearts. All of this came to an end with a kiss, when He was betrayed by one of those closest to Him.

Can you imagine their disillusionment when Jesus was placed in chains and beaten almost beyond human endurance? He was stripped of all dignity when they placed a crown of thorns on His head. There were those who knew that He was the Messiah, yet how could this be? Jesus appeared to be totally powerless.

Jesus had warned His disciples about what was going to

happen to Him: "Even as the Son of Man came not to be served but to serve and to give His life as a ransom for many." He had also said to them, "You will all fall away because of Me this night; for it is written, I will strike the shepherd, and the sheep of the flock will be scattered."

It appeared as if all had been lost, but, in fact, just the opposite was taking place. It was a new beginning for all of us. Unbeknownst to His followers, who had put their faith and trust in Him, they were about to witness an event that is unparalleled in all of history. Jesus was going to rise from the dead. When God created the world, He did so with His word, as He spoke the world into existence. Yet the power displayed at the creation pales in comparison to what took place in that tomb. God entered into death, swallowed it up, and came out the other side. There is no greater power than this.

Have there been times in your life when you felt abandoned by God? In moments of stress, fear, pain, and darkness, it seems as if God is nowhere to be found. I have certainly felt that way on more than one occasion. Frankly, I hate pain and suffering, and I find death repulsive. Even when I'm driving along the highway and I see a dead deer by the side of the road, I want to turn away from the sight. There is something very wrong about death. If this is true concerning the animal kingdom, it is little wonder that we shy away from death and suffering when it comes to ourselves and other human beings.

We are not alone in our feelings. Job was a man who was blessed by God with prosperity and health. He was one of the greatest men of his day. Suddenly, Job's future was completely reversed. He lost all of his possessions and his children, and his body was racked with disease. As if that were not enough, Job's three closest friends, who came to comfort him, insisted that suffering was a punishment for the sins in his life.

I think many of us can identify at one time or another with Jesus when He cried out, "My God, my God, why have you forsaken me?" What in the world is suffering all about? There is a mystery involved in suffering and death that I do not understand. When Job was subjected to all of the trials and suffering he endured, all that he wanted was an audience with God so he could ask, "Why am I suffering?" He could not understand what he was going through. Finally, when God did show up and spoke to Job, God did not answer any of Job's questions, but, in one sense, all of Job's questions were answered. I know how Job felt, and I cannot count the number of times I have been angry and disillusioned with God, but ever since I was ushered into His presence, I have been silenced. Once you have been in the presence of God, you will never again question His love, goodness, Glory, and majesty. His presence is simply the answer to our suffering.

There is one thing I do understand about suffering. Suffering is part of this fallen world, and God uses suffering in my life to bring me into a new place. I also know that God feels our suffering and pain more than we do, so, in one sense, He suffers with us. We cannot eliminate the mystery. Scott Peck, the brilliant psychiatrist and author, is one of my favorite people of all time. Concerning growth, Peck stated that all neurosis is the result of an unwillingness to suffer legitimate pain. There is a temporary death process, a letting go of the old, regarding our self-centered nature, that is involved in our growth and transformation.

Pride and our old nature put up a terrible fight and create their own way of trying to deal with pain. I was called to a hospital once when a man had just attempted suicide. He had shot himself in the stomach, because his wife had run away with another man. I talked to him at length and gave him the good news of Jesus Christ.

Several moments passed, and a sad look washed over his face. He finally said to me, "I know what you are saying is true, but I'm not willing to give up my life."

I could not believe my ears. Here was a man who had just attempted to kill himself, and he was not willing to turn his life over to Jesus to be healed. I have come to realize that this prideful nature resides in all of us, influencing us in a myriad of ways, which may seem insane to an outsider.

Not only do we have a prideful nature that wars against us in regard to love, but we are also filled with fear and laziness. It is essential that we overcome fear and laziness, in order to grow in love. Suffering is often the motivator that points a finger indicating that change needs to take place.

We are a culture that fears and runs away from pain. At the same time, we are filled with fear. Many people will run to a doctor at the drop of a hat, in order to stop any pain. How many people in our country get by in life by numbing them-selves on antidepressants and painkillers, so they don't need to change? In our attempts to avoid pain at any cost, we live with our fears and neuroses. Pain often points out that something is wrong and needs to change. I am not saying that we should delight in pain, nor am I saying that everyone should get off antidepressants and painkillers. I am saying, however, that if we attempt to avoid all suffering, we will die with our fears, and we will not grow in love.

There is something about suffering and death that brings things into perspective. A couple of years ago, a friend of mine died of cancer. Several years prior to his death, there was a lengthy period of time when I wanted nothing to do with him. He had insulted me, which hurt my pride. We finally made peace with each other, but, after his death, I felt a real sense of loss. All of the prideful hurt that I had felt seemed so insignificant and petty. There was no guilt involved in what I was feeling. It just seemed to me that many of the wars we wage and the grudges we hold onto become so insignificant when we're confronted with suffering and death. Suffering and death become a stripping-away process, in which the chaff is separated from the wheat, similar to the way that impurities are removed from gold. No one who is moving toward wholeness delights or takes pleasure in pain, but we can rest assured that God is using everything that happens in our lives for good, as He is preparing us to share in His Glory—the Glory of love without end.

11

Hall of Fame

My brother knows a man whose net worth is in the billions of dollars. This individual became very upset as it dawned on him that he could not take his wealth with him. Everything he had given his life to was going to stay behind after he died. He was not taking one penny with him. The pharaohs of Egypt erected giant pyramids in preparation for death. All kinds of valuables were placed in these elaborate tombs for their journeys into the afterlife. We can laugh at the absurdity of such notions, but the question remains, what will be our legacy when we depart this world? The only thing we take with us is love. Everything else remains behind.

There is a Hall of Fame for just about everything imaginable in this country. Recently, I was invited to a Super Bowl party, where I watched the big game. People talked about the football Hall of Fame as if it had lasting value. I mention this because I know God has a Hall of Fame, but what qualifies a person for God's role of honor is far different from what we Americans have created. Don't get me wrong—I love to fish, and I'm very competitive. By the way, do you know there is a fishing Hall of Fame? I love to fly around in my new Bass boat at seventy miles an hour in the beautiful bay on Lake Michigan. I know God delights in my joy of fishing, but I also realize there is a higher purpose for my being, because His goal for me is to grow in love. Of course, I can only speculate who might be in God's Hall of Fame, as a day is coming when we will stand in His presence to receive our reward.

Personally, as I speculate about that day, I think Harold might be a candidate for God's Hall of Fame. Not many people know Harold, but God does. Harold is a truck driver. He is one of those individuals who always seems to be in a good mood and who brings a breath of fresh air to life. He is funny, and he doesn't have a religious bone in his body. Harold does love the ladies and jokes around with them, but the truth is, he is harmless. Harold had a son with Down's syndrome, and the boy died in his early twenties. Harold's heart was broken, and he confessed to a close friend that he didn't care if he died as well. Most of us who have experienced real loss, especially when a loved one dies, know how that feels. Time passed, and Harold grew stronger. His wife asked him whether he would consider adopting another child.

"No way," he answered.

She persisted in her request, and again he said, "Not a chance." Then Harold stated, "The Lord would have to call me on the phone and ask me directly before I would consider adopting a child."

I could have warned Harold that saying this was a big mistake. He got the call! There were three little sisters involved, but the smallest, Mattie, had already been placed. Harold and his wife picked up the two girls, and they became part of his family. After eight months, they went before a judge to complete the adoption. While in front of the judge, Harold found out that the girls' little sister, Mattie, was not going to be adopted. The couple who had her now felt that they could not afford to raise her. When Harold discovered that she was going to be returned to the state system, he could not stop thinking about little Mattie. He petitioned his wife about adopting her.

"No way," she said. "Three would be too many."

Harold kept asking her, and, finally, his wife relented. "Okay, but you need to build me another bedroom and bathroom."

The deal was done. He took the money from his savings account and had the rooms built. A few days after they adopted little Mattie, she ran up, threw her arms around Harold's leg, and called him Daddy. Harold confesses that these three little girls are the joy and loves of his life, especially the little one. It seems no matter how tough his days are, little Mattie can always make him laugh. As a final note, one day Harold went to the mailbox to retrieve his mail and found a thick envelope. The postmark was from out of town. When he opened the envelope, it was full of cash. The amount was almost to the dollar what he'd had to spend on the two room additions. There was a note attached to the cash that read, "The Lord wanted me to send this money to you."

Harold's only comment was, "What kind of a person would send that much cash through the mail?" I could have told Harold what kind of person would do that: the same type of person that Harold is.

My friend Bo is another candidate for God's Hall of Fame, but I can assure you that he doesn't see himself that way and will be embarrassed when he reads this. Not only is Bo not religious, but he can be very irreligious at times. Bo is a semi-retired businessman, and at age seventy, he spends a great deal of time and money traveling to Africa to help build orphanages.

There are thousands of orphans in Africa, and many are orphans because their parents died of AIDS. About 40 percent of the children have AIDS. Bo has developed a genuine heart for these people, and the primary focus is on food distribution and holding healing services, where the miraculous is commonplace. God is working in their midst. Bo often tells me how poor many of these people are, including those in leadership roles. At the same time, needs are being met. He personally views his own involvement as a real blessing to him, with no sense of personal sacrifice. I definitely see him as a candidate for God's Hall of Fame.

You may be asking yourself, what in the world does this have to do with overcoming fear? The real disease most of us face is our own spiritual death, and nothing transforms us quicker than being delivered from ourselves. A movie produced several years ago illustrates this point. Titled *Patch Adams*, the movie stars Robin Williams. The movie begins in a mental institution, where Patch Adams has admitted himself, due to depression and a life without much meaning. As he starts helping his fellow inmates, he soon discovers that he is being delivered from himself. He decides to leave the hospital and enrolls in medical school. On graduation, he establishes an institution in which thousands of people are cared for and loved. His goal is not to see how much money he can store up for himself in this life, nor does he desire to be famous. His goal is to participate in the lives of people, in order to heal and encourage them. He is motivated by love—the kind of love that sets all of us free from ourselves and our fears.

Perhaps you will be led to prepare a meal for a sick friend or maybe give a stranger a cup of water when he is thirsty. You might be visiting those in prison or someone who feels very much alone. I do know that if you open yourself to the Holy

Spirit and what it means to love your neighbor as yourself, you are storing up treasures in Heaven for yourself. You will not be disappointed. You might even find yourself a candidate one day for God's Hall of Fame.

12

Where Do We Start?

Without faith, it is impossible to be connected to God. The reason this is true is that there is nothing we can do for God, except respond to what He is doing or has already done for us. God so loved the world that He gave His only Son, that whoever believes in Him will not perish but will have everlasting life. God saved us, and there is not one thing we can do to improve on that salvation. We can only respond to what He has done. When Jesus said, "It is finished!" it was finished.

Even though our salvation is complete, there is a process involved. We have been saved. We are being saved. We will be saved. Learning how to love is a daily process of growth that takes place until we leave this broken planet. After we shed this mortal shell, we will receive new bodies, and then our salvation will be complete. The entire process of the New Creation is one in which we respond in faith to what God is doing in us. How does this salvation work in our lives, and where do we start?

There is not one thing we can do to add to our salvation. God saved us from ourselves because He loves us. This is a simple truth that cannot be improved upon. There is another truth you will discover in your life, if you have entered into God's salvation. I call that truth the agony of faith. The simple truth of our salvation is going to be tested, and then life doesn't seem so simple any more. If you are a Christian and you are experiencing guilt and fear, your faith is being tested. If you feel God does not love and accept you for who you really are, you are being tested. If you think God is angry with you, you are being tested. As you grow in love through faith and come to really know who you are in God's love, those tests have no power over you and simply disappear.

God loves us, and He never uses guilt or fear to control our actions so that we will do His bidding. However, Satan does this. God loves us unconditionally. How you feel about that truth has nothing to do with the fact that it is a reality. When you trust in the unconditional love of God through faith, you will come to see and know that what I'm saying is true.

Practically speaking, the reason is that if you don't know that God loves you, you won't be able to trust Him, nor can you be honest with Him. I am absolutely amazed at those young men who flew the planes into the World Trade Center. Can you imagine submitting to a god in faith that would require you to do such a thing? I personally would tell that god to shove it up his ass. Who in their right mind could submit to such a loveless, angry, vengeful god? The only way you could submit to such a god is out of fear and arrogance, because you feel superior to those you are destroying. Trusting in that type of god is insane. How can one submit to a god when one has a greater sense of love than the god one worships? There are millions of people in our country who are worshipping such a god. Their religion condemns people whom they themselves would not condemn.

The God that I am writing about is love, and there is no

fear in His love. You will come to that conclusion only through faith, as you learn to trust Him and grow in love. If God is dealing with you or speaks to you, He will do so in love. If fear is threatening you, it is not of God.

What if you don't know God loves you? You may read this and might think that all of this sounds nice and good, but you don't feel that God loves you, and you are not about to play "Let's pretend." I can remember thinking the exact same way. I just knew I would never become a Christian, because there was no way I was going to fake it. Many of the people I knew were religious, and I believed they were playing games of "Let's pretend." Think nice thoughts. Do this and don't do that. Christians don't do that sort of thing.

One of my favorite comedians, who passed away several years ago, was a lifelong atheist. In one of his routines, he questions the religious god. "God seems to be an old man in a robe with a long white beard who wanders around Heaven with a list of ten things he doesn't want you to do. If he catches you doing any of these things, he judges you, punishes you, and then sends you to hell where you will be tormented for all eternity and—he loves you." I just knew I wouldn't be able to fake it or play "let's pretend," and that is when God found me. Trust me on this one point, if you feel this way: God does not want you faking it. Put Him to the test. Ask God specifically to help you be able to see yourself through His eyes. If He is really there, you need to know that He loves you.

If you're faking it, however, don't expect God to respond to you. You have to be real and honest with yourself. I know people who love to play the role of the victim: "Poor, pitiful me!" God knows everything about us, and He loves us, but He is not going to buy into a victim mentality, as we try to manipulate Him and others. We must assume responsibility for our own choices. If we want to be healed, we will be healed. If we want to be delivered from our fears, we will be delivered. But we have to want it.

When Jesus walked this earth, there was a man who came every day to a pool of water that was known for its healing powers. Other people carried him to the pool, because he was crippled. He had been coming to the pool for more than forty years. When Jesus first met this man, He asked him a very interesting question: "Do you want to be healed?" Every day for forty years the man had been coming to the pool, and Jesus asked him if he wanted to be healed. It is a great question, because many people have grown very comfortable playing the role of a victim. They come to the pool daily, never really expecting or wanting to be healed. We have to want to be healed before God shows up. He will not violate or take away our choice.

13

Power to Change

The truth about religion—and all religions are basically the same—is that everything can be explained in human terms. What I'm writing about cannot be explained in human terms. Try loving and forgiving people in your own capacity without the power of God. Try ridding yourself of the fears that stalk you on a daily basis without medicating yourself. Try filling your life with joy and peace when everything is crumbling around you. Try feeling safe and secure in a world that has gone mad.

I'm writing about the power of God in our lives, which is the power of love. This power is available to us if we simply ask. During the last few months, a good friend of mine seemed to be slipping away from our relationship. We would email and occasionally talk on the phone, but I sensed something was wrong. I could not tell what it was. I felt as if a negative spirit had come between us, so, finally, I sent her an email explaining my concerns. She called me on my cell phone soon after I emailed her. We talked for several minutes, but we were getting nowhere because we didn't see the issues the same way.

Our communications and perceptions were totally different. Something was blocking our connection, and I just could not see how we would work out our differences.

Finally, I just asked her if she would be willing to pray with me over the phone. She immediately agreed. I started by asking the Lord to examine my own heart to see whether anything in me was causing the problem. I wanted to know if I was the problem, so I could turn whatever it was over to the Lord. I then asked Him to restore our relationship and to take the negative spirit away. When it was my friend's time to pray, she basically said the same thing. We were both open to God's healing our relationship. After we finished praying, I mentioned to her that we should take a couple of days and then compare notes to see what the Lord revealed to us. It wasn't ten minutes after we hung up before the Lord spoke to me. He was very specific in what He said, and, at the same time, I could just feel His peace and warmth flowing over me. I had my answer.

I haven't heard from my friend, but healing and clarity have occurred within me, which produced a spirit of patience. There is a peace that surpasses understanding. The relationship will be restored. When you experience this type of supernatural power, you find a freedom within yourself that cannot be explained. God is actually creating something new in you that wasn't there yesterday. He increases your capacity for love by enabling you to see the person through His eyes, and, as He does this, your fears melt away. This is the life God is offering all of us, and it comes through the power of the Holy Spirit, which cannot be explained in human terms.

Don't think for one minute that I'm offering some formula to solve all of our problems. The only formula is our relationship with the Living God. The timing behind everything, in terms of growing in love, is based on our own personal relationship with Him. There are times when we will remain silent. There are times to speak. There are times to pray together, and there are times to separate. This is not about a life based on nice little ideas and empty platitudes. This is not about trying to mimic Jesus or anyone else. I am talking about a living, dynamic relationship with a God Who adores us and leads us by the Holy Spirit.

There are hundreds of things I don't have to think about or talk about with God. I have the freedom to be myself. There are mornings when I'm fishing out on the bay, and I witness a sunrise over beautiful Lake Michigan. I am literally speechless, as I behold the Glory of God in His creation. Often, I will simply stop fishing for a few minutes, while I sit spellbound. I may mumble something like, "Lord, You have really outdone Yourself this morning," as the sun breaks the early morning dawn of a new day. In moments like these, I know perfect freedom, doing what I love best in the majestic Glory of God's creation and being totally myself.

Contrast this with religion. There are religions where people must bow down several times a day, pointing in this direction or that. All religions have rules that must be kept, in order to please their angry god. Jesus did not come to make bad people good. Jesus came to make dead people alive. Religious people are in bondage to their religion. I am writing about the freedom to be yourself.

Bringing God into every situation in our lives where there is cause for concern is the way to personal freedom. We all have areas in our lives that give us cause for concern and produce fear. Bring each one of these concerns to the Lord.

Religion is man's way of attempting to reconnect with God, based on our own efforts. Religion is all about formulas and rules that only produce guilt and bondage. For those who appear to keep the rules, religion fosters an attitude of self-righteousness and superiority. The truth about religion is that none of it works, and nowhere do you find unconditional love. If you find yourself full of guilt, there is a good chance you have been strongly influenced by religion. Take that guilt to the Lord for healing. God never guilts us. God may reveal to us that we have a need to change because of a loveless or self-centered attitude. He wants us to grow in love. When God reveals this to us, He also empowers us to change. Guilt is all about me and my failure and disappointment with myself. Guilt is devoid of love, full of condemnation, and separated from God.

If you know Who God is and how much He loves you, you can bring any concern to Him. You can talk about your sex life, your finances, your marriage, your relationships, and all of your fears and concerns. He is not there to punish you in any way. You will not shock Him, because He knows everything about you. If He doesn't give you the power to change something about yourself that you want changed, He may want you to accept yourself for who you are. We often want something changed about ourselves because of what others think of us, and it's not really about us, but rather about our fears. God is not concerned whether we please others. He wants us to love others, but we cannot do that if we don't love ourselves. I have found in my own life that fear is the biggest culprit that keeps me from truly living. I know that if I were dying of cancer or some other dreadful disease, if I were completely free of fear, I would have no problems whatsoever. I would be at peace. Fear is the enemy.

The reason fear is the enemy is that it is separated from love. One of the main reasons we fear is that we fear death and punishment, which have already been swallowed up in Christ. As our fears are transformed into love, we really come to realize that we have nothing at all to fear. You will not arrive at this experience unless you discover this for yourself. Salvation is being reconnected to the God Who loves us and empowers us to grow in love.

What I find so ironic in my life is that when I experience real love, I am totally free to be me. In my old nature, separated from God, I believe just the opposite is true. In my old nature, I think real freedom comes from doing whatever I want, devoid of love, and I soon discover that I am in bondage.

As I look around me, I see that I'm not alone in my thinking. I see many unhappy people. We may be the richest country in the world and may own more things than anyone can possibly use, but I don't see this existence translating into anyone experiencing real peace and joy and having a genuine passion for life. I have lived in a million-dollar home with a breathtaking view; I have also lived in the jungles of Mexico and the foxholes of Vietnam. I've found that wherever I live or whatever I own, it does not produce real joy or happiness. I have experienced some of the best times in my life in very humble living conditions. When the Spirit of God lives in you, you will know that what I'm saying is true. The Fruits of the Spirit are love, joy, peace, patience, kindness, goodness, faithfulness, and self-control. When the Spirit resides in your life, you'll know what it means to be free.

Once you discover what I'm writing about, you'll find that God is your best friend. He is the only One Who loves you unconditionally. He wants the very best for you, and He loves you for who you are—and not based on His own needs. You don't have to hide from Him or play "let's pretend." He knows you far better than you know yourself. The choice to know Him is up to you.

14

Observations and Opinions

The first thirteen chapters of this work were inspired by the Holy Spirit's working in my life. When I make that statement, I don't mean that one day I just decided I would write about God and what I've learned about Him. It doesn't work that way for me. The writing chooses me; I do not choose the writing. The words come through me, and the inspiration comes from the Spirit of God. It is a living thing. Most of the time, I don't have a clue where we're going or what I'm going to write next. When I say "we," I mean the Holy Spirit and me. Often, while I'm writing a paragraph, I will come to understand a truth that I never saw in the past. It's as if the Holy Spirit is putting together the puzzle pieces of life.

There are times when I see the truth but find it difficult to come up with the right words. It's a Spirit "thing." The process is very mysterious to me, but I know it's a gift that comes to me. The authority for the writing is not based on my own ideas, but rather on what God has called me to write. The manifestation of this process does come through my personality, so it is not separated from me. I might express myself differently than you would, if given the same circumstances, but the truth would remain the same.

There are also times when I become frustrated with myself, because what I see sometimes seems to transcend language. I try to the best of my ability to make what is revealed to me as clear as possible. I do realize that all knowledge concerning God is part of a progressive revelation, and when the perfect comes, the imperfect will pass away. The apostle Paul wrote a letter to the church in Corinth and said, "If I speak in the tongues of men and of angels, but have not love, I am a noisy gong or clanging symbol. If I have prophetic powers and understand all mysteries and all knowledge, and if I have all faith, so to remove mountains, but have not love, I am nothing. If I give away all I have, and if I deliver my body to be burned, but have not love, I gain nothing." What Paul clearly says here is that love is the only thing that never ends, and in love, we find perfection.

This final Chapter 14 relates my thoughts about what I believe to be true, but I readily admit that speculation is involved. The authority for the remainder of this chapter is based on my own opinion. I am an ex-cop, and writing this chapter was similar to being a detective as he puts his case together. This chapter has to do with certain questions I've wondered about but really don't have answers. Having said that, I believe my conclusions are true.

I personally know Jesus Christ is the Son of God and the firstborn of the dead. He came to give us eternal life, and He is the Tree of Life. I believe He is the only way to salvation, but that has a very broad meaning for me. My question is, what about people who do not see or believe what I believe regarding Jesus? Love is as love does. I believe an atheist who truly loves is far more connected to Jesus than a self-righteous religious person who calls himself a Christian and hates and despises atheists. I believe there are Buddhists, Muslims, Hindus, and a host of people who do not know Jesus as the only way to salvation, yet if they are growing in love, they are in fact connected to Christ. I believe many Jewish people who are growing in love but don't accept Jesus as the Messiah will in the end be saved. I believe that after these people die and come face-to-face with Christ, they will accept Him for Who He is, the King of Kings, the Son of God.

There are two reasons that I believe this. First, I know Who God is. I know that God could care less about our theology or our belief systems. God is love. Jesus is love. The Holy Spirit is love. God does not damn anyone to Hell. People who are in Hell are there by their own choice. When we come face-to-face with our Creator, no one who truly loves or is looking for love will reject Him. Personally, I have no fear whatsoever for any loved one whom I know has gone to the other side. What the person happened to believe on this earth has little meaning to me. Some people I know may have a rude awakening, but I know that they are safe with God.

That brings me to my second reason. Several years ago, a good friend of mine, Skeet Puddy, died. This man had been like a father to me. We spent many hours fishing together and laughing together during the years we knew each other. On several occasions, I spoke about the Lord, but it was like talking to a brick wall. Skeet did not believe there was anything on the other side of this existence. When you are dead, you are dead. He died at age eighty-nine. After his death, I had an unsettled feeling in my spirit concerning this man. Weeks went by, and still the feeling persisted. I had no idea why I felt that way, but the feeling was undeniable.

One night, around three in the morning, a vision came to

me, and Skeet was ushered into my presence. He had a very confused look on his face, and I burst out laughing. Several times in my life the Holy Spirit has presented Himself (Herself) to me and I couldn't stop myself from laughing. In my vision, between laughs, I kept saying to Skeet, "I told you so, I told you so!" Then he was taken away from me. When I repeated to him, "I told you so," I was referring to the times I had tried to talk to him about eternal life with Christ. After that night, I knew Skeet was with the Lord, and he will be among the first people I meet. Where was Skeet during those weeks when I felt concerned about him? I don't have a clue. The Catholics' concept of Purgatory would be my best guess, but, really, I don't know. I do know he is okay, and I will see him one day in Glory. One thing I'm certain of is that you don't need to fear for any of the people you have loved and lost. God is love, and you can trust all of your loved ones with Him.

Evil People Need to Fear

What I find so ironic is that fearful people, in most cases, have nothing to fear, and evil people who should fear God have no fear at all. I believe Satan comes after people whom he knows have a genuine propensity for love. He uses fear in their lives to immobilize them and to keep them in a state of anxiety and bondage. For those who readily buy into Satan's lies, he anesthetizes them and energizes them, while filling them with prideful confidence about themselves. These people have no capacity for love. I have witnessed self-righteous, judgmental people who thrive on their condemnation of others and feel very smug and self-assured about their own lives and perspective. In reality, I believe these people have good cause to fear.

Several years ago, a man had a ministry, and one of his favorite sayings was "Turn or burn." He had a near-death experience, and, instead of finding the light, he found himself in Hell. When he was given a second chance, his new ministry became one of love and grace.

I have also witnessed people who enjoy hurting others and holding power over them as they destroy life and liveliness. These people feed off satanic energy, in order to fuel their appetites and lust. Such people have a union and a bond with Satan and have good cause to fear. God does not sentence anyone to Hell, but He will give people over to themselves, based on their own choices. Anyone who is heading in this direction has good cause to fear. Be not deceived, for God is not mocked. Whatsoever a man sows, that will he also reap. Hell is essentially a state of being we fashion for ourselves. Hell becomes eternal precisely because it turns into an immoveable state, as the person is consumed with the self, in regard to his or her choices.

We are created with free will, and that choice is real. God is not going to drag anyone kicking and screaming into Heaven. If a person has no desire to love and no desire to forgive and feeds off the misery and pain of others to satisfy his own appetite and desire, that person has good cause to fear—to fear being given over to himself or herself without love. Welcome to Hell.

Influencing Our World

We don't have the task of fixing the entire world, but rather stretching out to mend the part that is within our reach. It may be a small calming gesture that one soul can make to help another, reaching out somehow to aid a person in this suffering world. My mom was living in an assisted-living complex, and as we were making our way back to her apartment, we saw an elderly woman who seemed frozen to her walker. She had a look of terror on her face, as she cried for help. Mom simply walked up to the woman, put her arms around her, and assured her that everything was going to be all right. The woman became quiet and peaceful right before my eyes.

It is not given to us to know which acts, performed by whom, will create a touch of love that moves someone toward enduring goodness. We know that it does not take everyone on earth to bring love and peace, but only a few who are open to the Spirit of the Living God. Open yourselves daily to the Lord of life and ask Him what He would have you do. Listen for His quiet, gentle voice. You will discover that as you touch those around you, you, too, will be touched. And may God bless you and deliver you from all of your fears as you grow in love.

Randy

Special Thanks

Special thanks to Cecile Woda for her encouragement, art work for cover design, and typing and language skills. I also want to thank Patti Waldygo at Desert Sage Editorial Services whose commitment to excellence enhanced this work.

CPSIA information can be obtained
at www.ICGtesting.com
Printed in the USA
FSOW02n1450160516
20507FS